Contents

Meet the ducks

Quack! The ducks begin
their day on the farm.
Ducks swim in ponds
and streams. They waddle
across the grass.

Oklahoma State University, USA

raintree

a Capstone company — publishers for children

Raintree is an imprint of Capstone Global Library Limited, a company incorporated in England and Wales having its registered office at 264 Banbury Road, Oxford, OX2 7DY – Registered company number: 6695582

www.raintree.co.uk
myorders@raintree.co.uk

Printed and bound in China.

Editorial Credits
Michelle Hasselius, editor; Kayla Rossow, designer; Pam Mitsakos, media researcher;
Katy LaVigne, production specialist

ISBN 978 1 4747 2242 1 (hardback)
20 19 18 17 16
10 9 8 7 6 5 4 3 2 1

ISBN 978 1 4747 2266 7 (paperback)
21 20 19 18 17
10 9 8 7 6 5 4 3 2 1

British Library Cataloguing in Publication Data
A full catalogue record for this book is available from the British Library.

Acknowledgements
Shutterstock: Alta Oosthuizen, 6–7, Catherine Murray, 21, Daniel-Alvarez, 18–19, Eky Studio (back cover background), Elenamiv, 22 (background), Istvan Csak, 12–13, Jamie Rogers, 14–15, Kookkai_nak, 1 (background), kurt, 1, little_stardust, 17, Mariia Golovianko, 9, originalpunkt, 5, OZMedia cover; Thinkstock: SmaliarIryna, 11

The author would like to thank Dr Mark Z. Johnson for his invaluable help in the preparation of this book.

Every effort has been made to contact copyright holders of material reproduced in this book. Any omissions will be rectified in subsequent printings if notice is given to the publisher.

All the internet addresses (URLs) given in this book were valid at the time of going to press. However, due to the dynamic nature of the internet, some addresses may have changed, or sites may have changed or ceased to exist since publication. While the author and publisher regret any inconvenience this may cause readers, no responsibility for any such changes can be accepted by either the author or the publisher.

Ducks have long feathers. The outer feathers are waterproof to help ducks swim. The soft feathers underneath keep them warm.

Ducks clean and straighten
their feathers with their beaks.

More than 120 duck breeds

live around the world.

Only some live on farms.

Ducks can be white, black,

brown or other colours.

Adults and babies

Male and female ducks live on the farm. Males are called drakes. Females are called hens. Ducks can weigh 5 kilograms (11 pounds) or more. They live for 2 to 12 years.

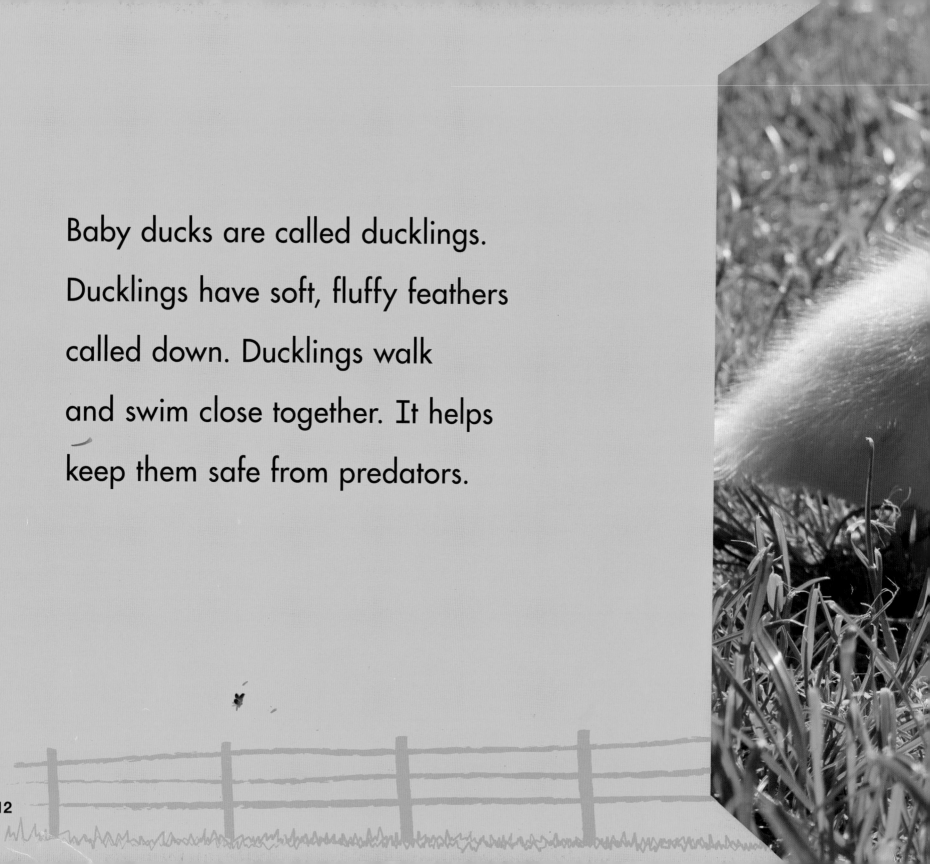

Baby ducks are called ducklings. Ducklings have soft, fluffy feathers called down. Ducklings walk and swim close together. It helps keep them safe from predators.

On the farm

Farmers keep ducks for their meat and eggs. Hens start laying eggs in spring. Duck eggs are larger than chicken eggs.

Ducks spend most of their time in water. They move their webbed feet like paddles to swim. Ducks can even swim in icy waters. Their feet don't get cold.

Time to eat

Ducks eat insects, plants and seeds. To reach food underwater, farm ducks lift their tails high in the air. Their heads dip into the water to grab the food.

Predators such as foxes eat
ducks. Farmers build pens with
high fences to keep them out.
Ducks stay safe on the farm.

Glossary

breed particular kind of animal within an animal group

paddle short, wide oar used to move and steer some boats

pen small, fenced-in area for animals

predator animal that hunts other animals for food

underwater under the surface of the water

waddle to take short steps while moving from side to side

waterproof able to keep water out

Read more

Animals on the Farm (Animals I Can See), Sian Smith (Raintree, 2015)

Ducks (Farmyard Friends), Maddie Gibbs (PowerKids Press, 2015)

Farm Animals: True or False? (True or False?), Daniel Nunn (Raintree, 2013)

Websites

www.dkfindout.com/uk/animals-and-nature/birds/waterfowl
Learn about different kinds of duck.

sciencekids.co.nz/sciencefacts/animals/duck.html
Read fun facts about ducks, play games and take quizzes.

Index